YORKTOUR: A WALK THROUGH THE WALLED CITY

WELCOME TRAVELLER

How did you get here today? If you came by train you will already have experienced the graceful, iron curves of the railway station, one of the great engineering projects of the Victorian age. Perhaps your first sight of York was the coach park, which was once the burying ground for victims of the plague (and hasn't become much pleasanter since, though even plague victims were not charged to use the toilets). It's not impossible that you sailed up river, like the Vikings; but more likely that you drove, approaching York the same way the Romans did, on a pre-historic route-way since resurfaced and renamed the A1.

Top: York's medieval guildhall and council chamber overlooking the River Ouse.
Above centre: The former London and North Eastern Railway headquarters shows the affluence of the railway age.
Above: Detail of a canopy at Jacob's Well in Trinity Lane – originally a 15th century pub sign.
Left: York Minster is the largest medieval gothic cathedral in Northern Europe.

But now that you're here, the chances are that you wish to make the most of the place but are at a loss where to start. The fortunate answer is that, in York, it is possible to start anywhere. In many other places the past lies buried; but in York the past is vibrant, visible and mostly above ground.

This is a city in which ancient and modern have always found a way to rub along together – it's the only place in England, for example, where you can see the remains of a Roman fortress, a ruined abbey, a royal palace and a scientific observatory not only within the same city, but within the same botanical garden. Across town, a Norman castle overlooks what appears to be a stately home, but was actually a prison.

Medieval shops are still in business, even if the merchandise has changed. You can buy shoes in half-timbered buildings or eat pizza in an 18th century ballroom.

Top: If York can be said to have a main entrance it would be Micklegate Bar, the south-facing arch through which the monarch traditionally approached the city.
Above: The city walls are open (weather permitting) 364 days a year.
Below: Apart from the cars, Petergate has barely altered from its appearance in a classic railway carriage print by Harry Tittensor from 1939.

This haphazard combination of historical styles means it is easy to get lost. But being lost in York is part of the fun; and for every blind alley there is always a glimpse of the city's crowning glory, the Minster, to navigate towards. Above all, York remains uniquely walkable. Having kept its medieval walls, the city remains on a medieval scale; and in the middle ages, people got around on foot.

The route mapped out in this book should take the average walker about two hours to complete at a moderate pace – longer, obviously, if you decide to stop off at the many places of worship or refreshment. If you add in a complete circuit of the walls you might wish to allow four to five hours in total – though be warned that exposure to York quickly becomes addictive. Many of those that live here are people who simply decided not to get back on the bus.

Top & above: The 12th century Walmgate Bar is unique among the four medieval gates in having retained its fortified front extension, or barbican. It was heavily damaged when the city was besieged during the English Civil War; but popular opposition prevented its demolition in the 1840s.

Left: The Minster viewed from the city walls. The earliest section of the wall enclosed a Roman fortress of some 50 acres, with a central basilica on the present site of the cathedral. The Vikings extended the Roman walls with a loop of earth-banks encompassing an area of approximately 263 acres, which broadly defines the outline of the city today.

EXHIBITION SQUARE

Above: William Etty (1787-1849) painter and conservationist.
Below: Old and new styles – St Leonard's reflected in the striking 1960s extension to the Theatre Royal.

To begin the tour, find a spot in front of the man on the plinth who has been rewarded with the best view in York. He can be found outside the art gallery in Exhibition Square, overlooking the fountain, and has earned the right to stand here because, without him, there may not have been very much left to look at.

The statue is that of a Victorian painter, William Etty. To state that Etty is the most famous artist to have come from York is not saying much, as his fleshy nudes have fallen some distance from contemporary taste. But it's worth noting that although the statue used to be holding a set of paint brushes (they mysteriously disappeared some time in the 1930s) below his right knee is an image of the medieval gateway on the opposite side of the road. The symbolism is significant given that Etty is now honoured less for his paintings than the fact that he was at the centre of a group of intellectuals (including the novelist Sir Walter Scott) who successfully petitioned Parliament to prevent the destruction of York's city walls.

Unthinkable as it may seem to us now, to the minds of Victorian industrialists and railway builders, the ancient ramparts were not a priceless piece of the nation's heritage. It was just an old wall that was getting in the way.

Right: Exhibition Square from a vintage postcard c.1900.
Previous page: York Railway Station was the largest in the world when completed in 1877.

A- 6055. YORK: BOOTHAM BAR.

With your back to Etty's statue it is possible to take in, at a single sweep, everything that he helped to preserve. Directly ahead of you is Bootham Bar, a Norman arch standing at the northern approach to the city on the site of a much older Roman gate.

Impressive though the bar may be, it is dwarfed by the west towers of the Minster rearing up behind. We will get to the cathedral eventually, but for now keep turning. To the right of the bar is the De Grey Rooms, a 19th century ballroom built for the officers of a cavalry regiment stationed in York. Next to that is the Theatre Royal, which has been in operation since the mid-18th century and has a Roman well and parts of a medieval hospital underneath the stage.

Facing the theatre is a crescent of Regency-style town-houses, built by a railway magnate who managed to knock down a 200 metre stretch of the city's defences before going any further. Behind the crescent, the King's Manor is a 13th century Abbot's house re-modelled in the 16th and 17th centuries to serve as a royal palace and now part of the University of York.

The Art Gallery alongside is a Victorian pastiche of Florentine Renaissance architecture and was the first public building in York to be lit by electricity.

Above left: King's Manor. Originally the house of the abbot of St Mary's, it was appropriated and extended by Henry VIII and now forms part of the University of York.

Left: St Leonard's Place. Completed in 1834, this Regency crescent came at considerable cost as it was built during a period when the complete demolition of the city walls was under consideration. Fortunately, only a 200-metre section was eventually sacrificed to build these fashionable townhouses.

To the right of the gallery is a section of the boundary wall of St Mary's Abbey, a great monastic house dissolved by Henry VIII. Follow the line of the wall to the red letter box, which brings us full circle; as it was the Romans who introduced the first postal service to Britain almost 2000 years ago.

Queen Margaret's Arch

Princess Margaret's Arch is named after the daughter of Henry VII, who stayed in York en route to her marriage to James IV of Scotland in 1503. Despite what the plaque *(right)* tells us, it was probably a cut-through for the Abbot of St Mary's to access the markets and ale houses of Bootham.

YORK MINSTER FROM BOOTHAM

We have just seen, in other words, 2000 years in 360 degrees, with examples from every phase of the city's development within a single turn. No other city in Britain presents quite such a panorama from a single spot – though as far as our walk through the walled city goes, this is only just the beginning…

St Mary's Abbey

Follow the path to the right of the art gallery, which opens out onto a piazza where ancient and modern meet. Behind you, the extension to the art gallery was created to house an important collection of 20th century ceramics (York is full of pots, from the Roman era to the present day). At the corner of the lawn is a circular tower known as the Hamlet of St Mary's. This was the only part of the city's defences ever to have been breached, when Parliamentarian forces blew it up during the English Civil War.

Apart from this, the walls did their job remarkably well and have only ever been broken on one other occasion, thanks to the imaginative power of Hollywood, when Mel Gibson was shown storming the city in the 1995 movie Braveheart. Though the 13th century Scottish freedom fighter William Wallace was real enough, he never made it this far south.

Top: The edible wood is planted with species of herbs and fruits from around the world, as well as the more locally-flourishing rhubarb.
Above: The Hamlet of St Mary's from a 19th century engraving.
Below: St Mary's Abbey.

The path winds through a garden known as the edible wood, as it contains herbs, fruits and vegetables from around the globe; including Schezuan chilli peppers, Japanese vines and, closer to home, a great deal of rhubarb which grows incredibly quickly in this part of the world. Pass through the gate in the corner which leads into the Museum Gardens, a green oasis containing the ruins of what was once one of the largest and richest of medieval monasteries.

St Mary's Abbey was founded 22 years after the Norman conquest, and was constructed under the supervision of William the Conqueror's son, known as Rufus – or William-the-Red – for his ruddy appearance. The money was raised by his kinsman Alan – also confusingly known as Rufus – who was one of the richest men in the kingdom. These red-faced Normans were by no means saintly men, though they lived in a world where piety had its price. Founding a monastery was the most direct means of purchasing a swift passage through purgatory to a prime spot in heaven.

The abbey was independent of the rest of York, with the monastery and town often in dispute over the right to hold markets and collect taxes. It was also widely suspected that the Benedictine monks who lived here were not wholly committed to a strict routine of meditation and prayer. The abbey became such a byword for decadence that a 'ryche abbot' of St Mary's features in one of the earliest ballads of Robin Hood.

Top: The grounds of St Mary's. This tranquil bowling green was briefly a battlefield during the English Civil War.
Above: the Geology of Yorkshire – a pebble mosaic in the Museum Gardens by Janette Ireland based on the work of William 'Strata' Smith (23 March 1769 – 28 August 1839), known as 'the father of English Geology.' He produced the first map of the geology of Britain.

Below: A medieval building site, from a series of manuscript illustrations. Note the use of a treadwheel crane, the figure of an architect holding an iron square, and the stonemason on the left using a plumbline.

This all came to a sudden end in 1534 when King Henry VIII severed relations with the Roman Catholic church, closed down the monasteries and seized possession of their wealth. Given that monks were responsible for tending to the sick, teaching children to read and giving charity to the poor, the dissolution of the monasteries had the devastating impact of closing all the schools, hospitals and social services at the same time.

As St Mary's was one of the largest foundations it was among the last to go, but in 1539 the abbot was given a pension of £200 and the monks a mere £5 annually. Henry's commissioners stripped the roof of its valuable lead, leaving wind, rain and looters to do the rest as the people of York helped themselves to the building stone for the next 300 years.

Above: Reconstruction of abbey stonework in the Yorkshire Museum.
Below: St Mary's in the mist.
Left: The Gardens of the Yorkshire Philosophical Society by J Storey c.1860. Note that a ferry connected the two towers on either side of the river until Lendal Bridge was constructed in 1863.
Courtesy of the Yorkshire Philosophical Society.

MULTANGULAR TOWER

From the abbey, continue your route past the mock-temple of the Yorkshire Museum, built in 1830 by William Wilkins, who also designed the National Gallery in London. The museum was created to house the collection of the Yorkshire Philosophical Society: the highlight of which is an Anglo-Saxon warrior's helmet, undisturbed for over 1200 years, until a workman discovered it in the shovel of his mechanical digger in 1982.

The grassy bank in front of the museum slopes down towards York's principal river, the Ouse, whose name derives from the Anglo-Saxon word for 'clear water'. The 8th century scholar Alcuin – who built a great library in York and possessed such an enquiring mind he is credited with the invention of the question mark – wrote a poem in praise of his home city. Alcuin writes of a cosmopolitan, mercantile settlement 'watered by the fish-rich Ouse that flows through flowery plains on either side'. It's probably fair to say that the Ouse must have been a great deal clearer and fish-rich in Alcuin's day than in ours.

Previous page: The rear of the Multangular Tower was once used by the curator of the Yorkshire Museum as a bear pit.
Top: The York Helmet.
Courtesy of York Museums Trust
Above: The York-born scholar Alcuin, acknowledged as one of the cleverest men in Christendom.
Left: The botanical gardens of the Yorkshire Museum were opened to the paying public in 1835 after the future Queen Victoria paid a visit.

The gardens are planted with specimens from around the world, though the dark, bushy evergreens you can see have always been here. These are yew trees; and two thousand years ago they were so plentiful that the city came to be named after them.

The Roman word for York was 'Eboracum', or place of the yew trees. Yew is a hardwood, good for creating palisades and weapons, which may explain why the Ninth Legion, marching north from Lincoln, chose to set up camp here in AD 71. The south west corner of the encampment can still be seen today: it is the imposing, ten-sided structure to the right of the museum known as the Multangular Tower.

York became the northern capital of Roman Britain (second only to London in the south) and flourished for approximately 350 years. At least three emperors came to York, emphasising the strategic importance of the wettest, coldest and most northerly outpost of an empire that stretched all the way from the new town of Eboracum to the Persian Gulf.

Top: The Multangular Tower formed the south west corner of the Roman fortress.
Above: A reconstruction of the Roman defences. Note the decorative lines of terracotta brickwork still visible in the surviving sections.
Right: Reclaimed sarcophagi within the borders of the Museum Gardens. The Roman roads outside the city gates are lined with ancient cemeteries.
Far right: A sprig of yew, after which the Romans named the city.
Near right: A Roman tile, found in York, with the stamp of the Ninth Legion.

When the Roman empire began to crumble at the beginning of the fifth century, the stone fortress crumbled as well. For the next four hundred years Anglo-Saxon settlers lived among the ruins of the Roman city, which they called Eoforwic (place names in England ending with the suffix 'wic' or 'wich' indicate an Anglo-Saxon trading settlement).

In 866 the town was attacked and colonised by Vikings and the name mutated into the Scandinavian 'Jorvik' from which the modern name derives. With the exception of a few early stone churches, neither Saxon nor Viking architecture was built to last and their legacy is mostly buried beneath the ground. But the next wave of invaders – the Normans – revived Roman construction methods with a vengeance.

Within two years of the conquest in 1066 the city was comprehensively razed and forcibly rebuilt in stone, during which time York gained two castles (one of which survives), an immense cathedral and the equally large abbey whose ruins we have just seen.

But wherever the Roman fortifications existed in a practical state of repair, the Norman builders took advantage. The Multangular Tower is an example of Norman invaders finishing off a job that Roman invaders had started over 1000 years earlier – the change in size and colour of the stonework at the top gives it the mismatched appearance of a newly-capped tooth.

Above right: The structure known as the 'Anglian Tower' can be found behind the Multangular Tower. Opinion is divided as to whether it was a late-Roman addition or an early Anglo-Saxon repair.
Centre right: Layers of history.
Bottom right: St Leonard's Hospital was founded in the 10th century. Its 200 beds made it one of the largest in England.

THE KING'S MANOR

Follow the path that runs through the rockery to the left-hand side of the Multangular Tower. The route soon becomes sandwiched between an embankment of the city wall on one side and a substantial stone building known as the King's Manor on the other. Originally this was the house of the abbot of St Mary's (medieval abbots were accustomed to living in the grand style) until Henry VIII appropriated it for himself.

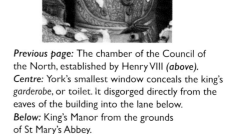

Previous page: The chamber of the Council of the North, established by Henry VIII *(above)*.
Centre: York's smallest window conceals the king's *garderobe*, or toilet. It disgorged directly from the eaves of the building into the lane below.
Below: King's Manor from the grounds of St Mary's Abbey.

Henry had no great fondness for York, nor the people of York for him. In 1536 the city played a key part in a mass-protest movement against the closure of the monasteries known as the *Pilgrimage of Grace.* This was more of a popular uprising than a pilgrimage, led by a charismatic Yorkshire lawyer known as Robert Aske, who demanded that all the displaced monks and nuns be re-instated. Henry defused the situation by promising concessions to the protestors, then arrested Aske, who was strung up in a gibbet from the walls of York castle and left to die of exposure and starvation. The message of this deterrent was simple: don't Aske.

Henry came to York in 1541 to exact an official apology from the city's mayor and aldermen, who declared themselves to be 'repentant from the bottom of their stomachs' before handing over a sizeable gift of £100 for the king and £40 for his fifth queen, Catherine Howard.

It was during their stay at the King's Manor that Catherine began making secret visits to the bedroom of her husband's personal valet, Thomas Culpepper (an indiscretion for which both were to lose their heads).

The coat of arms above the main entrance to the King's Manor belongs to Charles I, who based his command here during the English Civil Wars of 1642-51. York was a staunchly Royalist city when it came under siege by Parliamentarian forces in 1644. Under normal circumstances, the victorious roundheads would have been expected to run rampage, destroying religious icons and smashing the city's priceless stained glass. That this didn't happen was due to the unusual historical circumstance of the Parliamentary commander, Sir Thomas Fairfax, besieging his home town. Fairfax decreed, once the city had fallen, that all its buildings and citizens be spared.

Top: The coat of arms of Charles I, who took refuge in the King's Manor during the English Civil War.
Above: Catherine Howard (1523-1542) unlucky fifth wife of Henry VIII.
Right: Sir Thomas Fairfax (1612-1671) the Yorkshire Parliamentarian who first besieged, then spared the city.
Below: The Manor gardens from a 19th century watercolour.

Though the city escaped through the good graces of Fairfax, it is worth noting that York has a very poor record predicting the outcome of civil conflict. During the Glorious Revolution of 1688, the city pledged its support to the Catholic James II, until the King's Manor was captured on behalf of William of Orange. And during the unseemly baronial land-grab known as the Wars of the Roses, York initially remained loyal to the Lancastrian king Henry VI before pledging allegiance to the Yorkist Richard III; thus gaining the curious distinction of having switched sides in order to back the loser twice.

BOOTHAM BAR

The path alongside the King's Manor emerges back out into Exhibition Square. It's now time to cross the road and enter the city through Bootham Bar, the oldest of York's four ancient gateways. There has been an entrance here for almost 2000 years, since it formed the northern approach to the legionary fortress. The arch you can see today dates from the 11th century, and is partly constructed from pieces of recycled Roman coffins. The upper portions of the bar were extended in the 14th and 15th centuries; and the statues on top (actually modern replacements) represent, from left to right, the masons, who built the walls; the mayors, who financed them; and the knights, who came to their defence.

Within England, only Chester retains a comparable set of medieval walls (whose are the finest remains a matter of dispute: Chester's are more complete, but at two-and-three-quarter miles, York's are longer). The city walls now form York's most spectacular public footpath; and it is still possible to make a full circuit with two significant exceptions. A two-hundred metre section was demolished in the 19th century between Bootham Bar and the river to create the crescent of townhouses leading into Exhibition Square. And there is a gap on the north eastern perimeter where an impenetrable marsh made the building of a defensive wall both impossible and unnecessary. Today this little-explored quarter is fringed with a ribbon of auto-parts centres and supermarkets that are no less effective at putting visitors off.

Previous page: A clear day in the Museum Gardens.
Top and centre: Bootham Bar – the city's gateway to the North, built to withstand Scots.
Bottom: The walls in Autumn.

A complete tour of the walls is beyond the scope of this guide: but the most satisfying and picturesque section can be accessed by ascending the steps at Bootham Bar. From here the walls overlook the Minster close, directly tracing the line of the Roman fortress whose foundations occasionally break the surface of the grass bank below.

Why the sudden need for so much solidity? Part of the answer lay with the ever-present threat of the Scots, against whom seemingly endless campaigns were launched from York. An un-repealed medieval statute theoretically still permits any citizen to shoot an unauthorised Scotsman with a bow and arrow. But the walls were ultimately of less use for defence than as an expression of civic pride. To the approaching visitor, the spires and towers of the forty-four parish churches must have looked like the masts of sailing boats clustered round the giant mother-ship of the Minster.

Above: The steep embankments were the work of the Vikings, who buried what was left of the Roman defences when they took control of the city in the 9th century. Every year, in early spring, these uncompromising earthworks are beautified with a decidedly un-Viking spray of daffodils. The stone ramparts you can see today were mostly raised during the long reign of Henry III (1216-1272), who promoted a construction boom in York by offering tax incentives to build walls.

Below: 'The South-East Prospect of the City of York' by Samuel & Nathaniel Buck, published in 1745. York Museums Trust

But more importantly, the walls were good for business. Like all the bars, Bootham once had an elongated front-extension, known as a barbican (only one of which survives intact, at Walmgate Bar on the opposite side of town). Barbicans functioned as a kind of fortified holding-pen; and though it is colourful to imagine them being used to pour boiling oil and arrows onto helpless invaders trapped below, they more effectively functioned as customs posts, exacting taxes from any trader entering or leaving the city with something to declare.

YORK MINSTER

Right angles are rare in York, but Bootham Bar leads into High Peter-gate, a relatively straight road that intersects after a few hundred yards with the even-straighter Stonegate. The regularity of these roads is due to their Roman origin – where they meet marks the position of the legionary headquarters, or principia. It is at this significant crossroads that the Minster stands today.

This area has been York's spiritual heart for 2000 years and at least four cathedrals have occupied this site. A question often asked is why the building is known as the Minster? Part of the answer lies in the fact that its official title – the Cathedral and Metropolitical Church of St Peter in York – does not roll quite so easily off the tongue. But the term 'minster' refers to its 7th century origins as a missionary church.

The first Minster was a modest wooden baptistry built in 627 in order for the heathen King Edwin of Northumbria to receive the Christian faith (Edwin was betrothed to marry a Christian princess from Kent and his conversion was part of the deal). The wooden chapel was replaced by a stone structure that was destroyed first by the Vikings in the 9th century; and again by the Normans two hundred years later. The Normans established their dominance by sacking York and building a Romanesque cathedral on a scale that had never been seen before.

Top: York Minster: Roman, Saxon, Viking and Norman churches have all occupied this site.
Above: The 'Heart of Yorkshire' illuminates the nave.
Above left: A woodcut image of York Minster as depicted in the first map of the city, produced by John Speed around 1610 *(below)*. This wasn't how the Minster actually appeared in the early 17th century: it is more of a generalised symbol designating 'very large church'.
Interior photos © Chapter of York: reproduced by kind permission.

Yet by the year 1220, the Archbishops of York had become engaged in a furious building race with their great rivals in Canterbury; and the huge Norman church was no longer seen as quite huge enough. Work was initiated on a massive rebuilding programme, in the fashionable new French style, that grew to become the largest gothic cathedral in northern Europe.

This final transformation took over 250 years to complete. The present Minster, which was finally consecrated in 1472, is laid out like a giant encyclopaedia of gothic building styles. The first phase – known as 'Early English' – is visible in the transepts, whose most famous feature, the Five Sisters, is England's oldest and most enigmatic stained glass window.

The Five Sisters is unusual for a medieval window in that it contains no pictures or Biblical images, but is based on a sequence of repetitive geometric patterns. These have become obscured over time, but are clearly influenced by Islamic design. The quintet of narrow, spear-shaped arches is similarly derived from mosque architecture, introduced to Europe at the time of the Crusades. It is a curious twist of architectural development that Christian soldiers stole the innovations of the infidel for use in their own cathedrals.

The seventy years or so which separates the Five Sisters from the West Window at the far end of the nave is almost like the world of monochrome being replaced by the arrival of technicolour.

Top left: The gilded dragon is one of the Minster's great enigmas.
It may have functioned as part of a pulley system for lifting a font or reliquary cover,
but significantly faces a statue of Saint George *(centre left)* on the opposite side of the nave.
Below left: Completed around 1260 and inspired by Islamic design, the Five Sisters
is the largest medieval grisaille window in the world.
Interior photos © Chapter of York: reproduced by kind permission.

The West Window was completed in the 1330s during the height of the 'Decorated' phase of gothic building, during which time windows evolved into giant tapestries of light topped with delicate sprays of stone tracery. The romantic emblem at the apex of the West Window is a virtuoso example of the Decorated style that has come to be known as the Heart of Yorkshire.

Left: The east end of the Minster underwent major restoration between 2010-15 and contains the largest expanse of medieval stained glass in the world.
Above: Fire damaged medieval roof bosses, destroyed on the night of 9th July 1984 when a fire, believed to be caused by a lightning strike, caused the roof timbers of the south transept to collapse *(below)* Miraculously, the Rose Window *(top)* survived the heat.
Interior photos © Chapter of York: reproduced by kind permission.

The east end of the Minster was the last phase to be completed, in the style known as 'Perpendicular' gothic. This arm of the cathedral marks a sudden change to a more upright, austere style that may reflect a change in attitudes following the first outbreak of the Black Death from 1348-50, during which six out of every ten members of the population died. To the medieval worshipper, the catastrophe must have seemed to be the end of the world, whose inescapable prophecy appears in the Great East Window, the Minster's largest and most harrowing work of art.

The Great East Window forms the transcendent backdrop to the entire cathedral, and is the masterpiece of the medieval glass painter John Thornton of Coventry. Thornton was paid a fee of £56, plus a £10 bonus for completing on time as he accomplished the work in only three years between 1405 and 1408.

Thornton's commission, to give graphic form to the horrors described in the Book of Revelation, was arguably the most ambitious single-handed work of religious design before Michelangelo began work on the Sistine Chapel 100 years later. For the original viewer, Thornton's vision of the apocalypse must have been quite terrifying – the window is a kaleidoscopic nightmare of burning skies and poisoned rivers that seems to foretell the ecological catastrophe of our own times. The completion of a £20 million restoration programme in 2016 returned the glass to a state of iridescence not seen since Thornton first installed it over 600 years ago.

Top: St John the Evangelist receives the Book of Revelation: a detail from the Great East Window.
Centre: The seven-headed beast of the Apocalypse appears several times in John Thornton's illuminated vision of the end of the world.
Below and right: The frieze of kings, carved around 1450, separates the nave from the choir. This royal portrait gallery represents the fifteen monarchs who held the throne throughout the construction of the Minster from William the Conqueror to Henry VI.

Interior photos © Chapter of York: reproduced by kind permission.

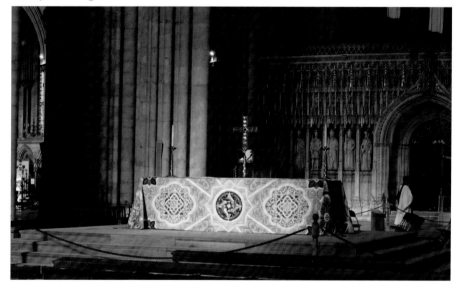

AROUND THE MINSTER

A circuit through Dean's Park - the green space that fringes the north side of the Minster – enables you to appreciate the sheer scale of the 1/10th mile-long cathedral. The park was once the site of the archbishop's palace, of which only a row of broken arches and the chapel in the corner remains (it now houses the Minster library). Since 1241, the Archbishops of York have occupied a palatial residence three miles upstream at the village of Bishopthorpe.

Opposite the gate leading out of the east side of the park, a forlorn stone statue – popularly known as Mr Blobby – sits imprisoned behind a set of iron railings, having been put into retirement after 600 years on the east face of the Minster. This giant figure of St Peter was so badly weathered as to be almost completely unrecognisable and was replaced during the restoration work completed in 2015. The new St Peter was carved by the Minster masons using only hand-tools and techniques available to their medieval predecessor, though they had the benefit of hydraulic lifts and modern scaffolding to hoist the seven-foot, two-tonne figure thirty metres above the ground.

Top left: The original St Peter, retired after 600 years on the east face of the Minster. Since Roman times, limestone has been quarried locally and transported by river from the town of Tadcaster. These quarries still supply stone for the cathedral today, though the two-metre block required for the new St Peter (**left centre**) had to be imported from France.

Left and centre: Dean's Park contains the chapel of the medieval archbishop's palace, now the Minster Library. Among the treasures of this collection is an extremely rare copy of the so-called 'Wicked' Bible of 1631 – an edition which, due to a printing error, omitted the word 'not' and gives the Seventh Commandment as: 'Thou shalt commit adultery'.

Despite its name, St William's College – the half-timbered building behind the east end of the cathedral – was never an educational establishment, but a secure dormitory founded to keep unruly clerics under lock and key. Until the 16th century it was common for wealthy donors to endow a private chapel, or chantry, in the Minster. The chantry priests were often to be found loitering around the red-light district or causing chaos with their arch-rivals, the vicars choral, who deputised for rich, absentee canons who rarely attended the Minster in person.

The remains of the vicars' choral residence can be glimpsed through the alleyway on the opposite side of the road to St William's College. Physical confrontations between vicars choral and chantry priests became so common in this part of town that a covered footbridge had to be constructed to keep them apart.

Top: A fragment of the first Archbishop's palace.
Above: Monk Bar – the tallest of the city gates.
Below and left: St William's College.

The bridge – which no longer exists – spanned Goodramgate, named after the Viking king Guthrum, which curves down towards Monk Bar, the tallest and most heavily fortified of the medieval gateways. The upper stories of the bar were extended by Richard III, who is often associated with the unscrupulous hunchback of Shakespeare's play, but was a popular figure in York since he halved the city's taxes and wished to be buried in the Minster.

The reinforcements sent from York to the Battle of Bosworth in 1485 arrived too late; and the council record notes that the king 'was most grievously and treacherously slain to the great heaviness of this city'. In September 2012 a skeleton showing signs of battle wounds and slight curvature of the spine was exhumed from beneath a car park in Leicester. This was also to the great heaviness of the citizens of York, who mounted an unsuccessful legal challenge to bring the bones back north.

Top: The upper stories of Monk Bar are the legacy of Richard III *(above)*.

Right: The Treasurer's House is medieval in origin but was almost entirely rebuilt in the early 17th Century when James I came to visit. It stands on the site of a former Roman road; in 1953 a plumber's apprentice reported seeing a phantom column of the 9th Legion marching through the cellar.

STONEGATE

Of all the invasions York has experienced over the centuries - Roman, Viking, Norman, Puritan - none has been more dangerous or destructive than the invasion of the motor car. Traffic was allowed to pass within a few metres of the Minster until as recently as 1991, though now the south side is bounded by a light and airy piazza from which cars are excluded (but not cyclists, who tend to relive the year the Tour de France passed through York in 2014, so do take care when making your way across).

On the far side of the piazza stands a solitary Roman column, excavated from beneath the Minster at the end of the 1960s when it was discovered that the entire weight of the central tower was resting on Roman foundations. The results of the engineering work that saved the Minster from collapse are visible in the undercroft where, amid the Roman, Norman and medieval layers, four massive concrete collars counteract 4000 tonnes of downward thrust, approximately the same force as a space rocket taking off.

Opposite the column sits a modern likeness of a Roman emperor deep in thought. This is Constantine, the first Christian emperor, who was proclaimed in York in the year 306. If you look closely you will notice that the tip of his sword is broken. The weapon has been modified into the form of a crucifix, representing the moment at which a minor, persecuted sect became the dominant religion of the western world.

Top left: Stonegate from St Helen's Square – the main axis of Roman York.
Centre: A Roman column, excavated from beneath the Minster, marks the site of the basilica in which Constantine *(left)* was proclaimed emperor.

Shoulder-to-shoulder with the cathedral stands St Michael-le-Belfry, one of York's most impressive parish churches. There were over forty parish churches in medieval York – something of a super-abundance considering that cities such as Leeds and Hull had only one. St Michael-le-Belfry is notable for an entry in the baptismal record for April 13 1570, in which the future gunpowder plotter Guy Fawkes was born into the Anglican faith (and would grow up doing his best to destroy it).

Minster Gates, the short street opposite the south door of the cathedral, is now gate-less but indicates that until the 19th century the Minster was tightly enclosed within its own walled compound. Look up above the facade of the shop on the right: a colourful statue of Minerva, the Roman goddess of wisdom, surveys what used to be the medieval quarter of stationers, printers and pen-pushers.

Top: St Michael-le-Belfry.
Left: The goddess Minerva presides over Stonegate, the street of printers and booksellers *(above)*.
Below: Three of the gunpowder plotters, John and Christopher Wright and – most famously – Guy Fawkes, came from York.

Robert Winter   Christopher Wright   Iohn Wright   Thomas Percy   Guido Fawkes   Robert Catesby   Thomas Winter

Further evidence of this activity can be found along Stonegate, beneath the 17th century sign for the Starre Inn, where a diminutive red devil guards the entrance to an alley known as Coffee Yard. York's first newspaper was produced here; even today, the youngest apprentice in a printer's workshop is known as the 'printer's devil'.

If time permits, it's worth trying the door to number 52A on the opposite side of the road. It leads to the parish hall of St Michael-le-Belfry, but is chiefly notable for a yard containing the remnants of a Norman house. Very little domestic architecture of the post-conquest period survives in England. But York's Norman house is a phantom intimation of how the rich and powerful lived around the year 1180.

Top: Fragments of a Norman residence.
Above: St Helen's Square, named after the mother of Constantine.
Left: Angel or devil? A 17th century ship's carving shows a split personality – winged angel on one side, finned mermaid on the other.
Top right: The Red Devil, the traditional sign of a printer's shop.
Right: Stonegate remains one of York's finest shopping streets.

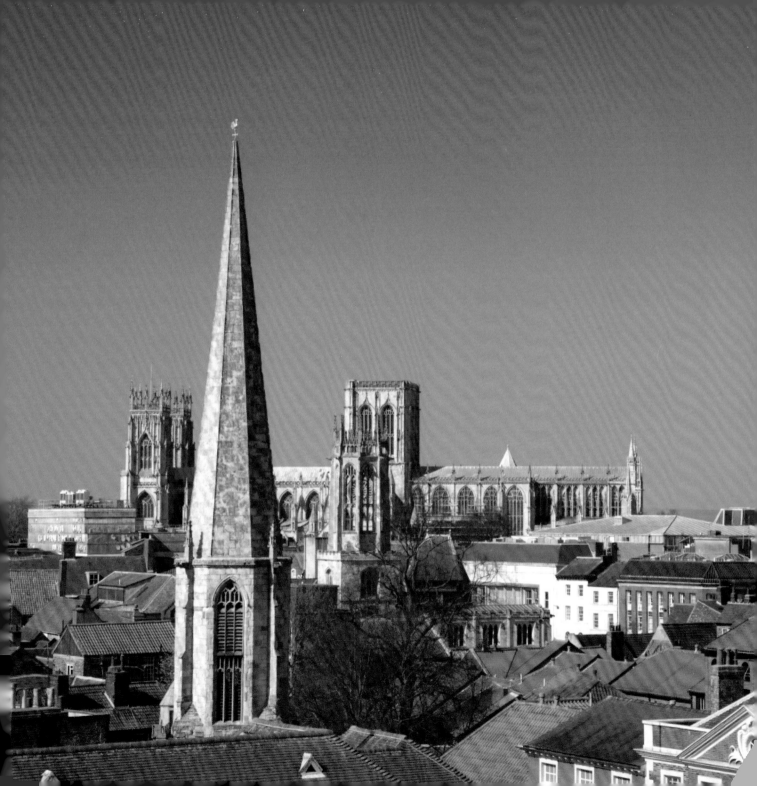

BARLEY HALL TO THE SHAMBLES

Exploring the heart of medieval York is like peeling back layers of historical wallpaper. Coffee Yard is a case in point: in the 19th century, this passageway led to the middle of a Victorian slum. It was not until the 1980s, when the derelict tenements were cleared, that the Victorian brickwork was found to conceal the timbered facade of a fine, 14th-century manor house. It has now been extensively restored and renamed Barley Hall by the York Archaeological Trust, which returned the building to its appearance at about the time it became the property of William Snawsell, Lord Mayor of York and prominent supporter of Richard III, who most likely entertained the king here during the Wars of the Roses.

Beyond this point, anyone above average height is advised to mind their head. Central York contains a warren of low, narrow passageways referred to by locals (who are expected to know the difference) as alleys, snickets and ginnels. The distinction between them is not immediately apparent – if confused, it's best to fall back on the catch-all term coined by the local historian and illustrator Mark W. Jones for his highly recommended guide, *A Walk Around the Snickleways of York*.

This particular Snickleway emerges into the attractively cobbled Grape Lane (originally a street of ill-repute called Grope Lane, where chantry priests were notorious for causing disturbance). Proceed directly ahead onto Swinegate where, as the name suggests, you join medieval York's original pig run.

Top: The west towers of the Minster viewed from High Petergate.
Above: Barley Hall – a surprising rediscovery.
Below: Beneath Swinegate a system of Roman sewers and under-floor heating for a bathhouse remains remarkably intact.

Had you been here in the middle of the 14th century it would have been impossible not to notice the odour. Indeed, York was so pungent that Edward III issued a royal proclamation 'detesting the abominable smell abounding in the city'. The epicentre of the stink was to be found in the dark, narrow channel of medieval properties known as the Shambles.

Today the Shambles is admired as one of the best-preserved medieval streets in the world. In the 14th and 15th centuries it was an open-air abattoir in which all the premises belonged to butchers. You can still see the original meat-hooks above the oldest properties on the left hand side; as well as the substantial window ledges, known as 'shammels'. This was the Anglo-Saxon term for a chopping-block – screen out the tea-rooms and tourists for a moment and try to imagine the whole street as an obnoxious midden of haggling housewives and terrified animals.

The house at number 35 contains the shrine of York's most famous Catholic martyr, Margaret Clitherow, who was led to Ouse Bridge and crushed to death in 1586 for giving refuge to Catholic priests. Margaret was canonised in 1970, though it's now believed that the priests were concealed in the house opposite, as the street numbering has been re-ordered over time. And you will have to decide for yourself which of the shops inspired the place where, in the first Harry Potter film, a certain boy wizard purchased his school supplies.

Above: The Shambles, as it appeared in a postcard view c.1910.
Centre right: Originally the street of butchers, the merchandise is now considerably more diverse.
. *Right:* The martyrdom of Margaret Clitherow – pressed to death for concealing Catholic priests.

MERCHANT ADVENTURERS TO THE VIKING MARKET

Directly opposite the end of the Shambles stands one of York's grandest half-timbered buildings. Its most illustrious occupant was Thomas Herbert, a 17th century adventurer who sailed as far as Madagascar and sketched one of the first known images of a dodo. During the Civil War he was Gentleman of the Royal Bedchamber; and though technically Charles I's jailer, he became increasingly fond of the old king, whose last action before laying his head on the block in 1649 was to hand Herbert his cloak as a reward.

Rather than admiring Herbert's house, however, turn your attention to the pizza restaurant immediately next door. In the 1840s this was a grocer's shop belonging to the Rowntree family, who developed York's most successful business. Joseph Rowntree was a Quaker, and an advocate of temperance, who hoped the working classes might abandon alcohol in favour of his bitter, gritty brand of drinking chocolate (in the 19th century, cocoa was marketed as a health food).

Above: The Herbert House.
Below: Pavement as it appeared at the end of the 19th century. To the right of Sir Thomas Herbert's house (covered in Victorian plaster) is the grocer's shop from which Joseph Rowntree founded his chocolate empire.
Explore York Libraries & Archives

Though he never put any brewers out of business, the cocoa empire took off and in 1869 Rowntree established a vast confectionery factory to the east of the city. This is still in operation today - thanks largely to the popularity of a biscuit known originally as Rowntree's Chocolate Crisp, though it only really took off once it had been rebranded as the KitKat. Every five minutes the York factory produces enough KitKats to pile higher than the Eiffel Tower, though the Rowntree name has disappeared from the wrapper as Nestlé took over the company in 1998.

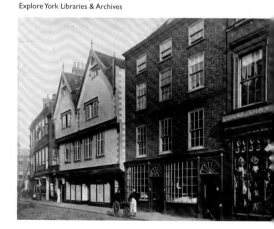

Top: The arms of the Merchant Adventurers above the entrance to their hall *(centre)*. *Above:* Foss Bridge spans the smaller of York's two rivers.

Time for another spot of snickleway navigation. Head down the alley alongside the Herbert House, known as Lady Peckitt's Yard, which turns at a right angle before emerging onto Fossgate. Take a right turn here and just before the road rises to a hump over the river, look for an elaborate coat of arms showing two winged horses. This marks the entrance to the Merchant Adventurers' Hall.

You have now arrived at the heart of the medieval financial district. The Merchant Adventurers formed the city's richest and most powerful trade organisation, or guild; and made their money speculating on the international wool trade. They were investors rather than actual adventurers, though the wealth they accumulated through foreign trade was advertised by the magnificence of their headquarters, which opened in 1357.

Leave the Merchants' precinct through the iron gates on the opposite side of the hall. A left turn leads you towards the smaller of York's two rivers, the Foss, which is so narrow and placid it is often mistaken for a canal. In fact this stretch was made navigable in the 19th century in order to improve access to Rowntree's cocoa warehouse.

Cross the road and follow the bank of the Foss where it passes behind a modern shopping development. Though the back of the Coppergate Centre is far from York's most attractive sight, it has huge historical significance, as the laying of foundations in the 1980s revealed the original Viking settlement of Jorvik.

The Vikings conquered York on All Soul's Day 866, sailing up the Ouse in a stealth attack that must have been as devastating to the Anglo-Saxon population as 9/11 or Pearl Harbour. Yet the Vikings did not just sack York, they settled here; adopting Christianity and transforming from a race of heathen warriors into a nation of urban shopkeepers. Their workshops and living quarters can be visited five metres beneath the ground at the world-famous Jorvik Viking Museum, which contains a wealth of astonishingly-preserved 10th century artefacts including leather goods, clothes, shoes and kitchenware. Interestingly, the shopping centre on top still trades in all of the above, which goes to prove that nothing ever really changes in York.

Above: The Blue Bridge stands at the confluence of the rivers Ouse and Foss. The Viking trading settlement nestled between the fork in the two rivers.

Left: The heart of commerce, old and new. Viking Jorvik lies directly beneath Coppergate, seen on the left. In the middle ages, when the church of All Saints was built, this was the site of the market. The Edwardian bank on the right dates from 1901 and is one of York's finest terracotta buildings.

PEASHOLME
GREEN

THE EYE OF YORK

Following the Norman conquest, it would not have been possible to access this part of town unless you were prepared to swim. Today the Foss only floods by accident – which happened to devastating effect in the winter of 2015 – but was done so on purpose by William the Conqueror in 1068 to create a defensive moat for the castle that emerges on the right.

It took two years following the invasion of 1066 for the Normans to completely subdue the north. They achieved it with a brutal policy of burning all the villages, homesteads and farmland between York and the Scottish border, causing an estimated 100,000 people to die of starvation. York itself was laid to waste and rebuilt as a Norman citadel with two castles guarding the entrance on either side of the river. On the south bank of the Ouse, only an overgrown mound remains. But Clifford's Tower, which has a four-lobed quatrefoil design rare outside France, served for several centuries as the city's mint, prison, treasury and most-feared landmark.

Top: Clifford's Tower only gained its present name after a Sir Roger Clifford was hanged here in 1322.
Above: The Assize Courts (now York Crown Court) were designed by John Carr and opened in 1777. Visiting judges were traditionally presented with bunches of herbs by the Lady Mayoress to counter the scent of felons.
Below left: The view from Clifford's Tower looking north west towards the Magistrates Court and Bishophill.
Below: The clock tower on the Castle Museum, originally the Debtors' Prison.

The Castle and Cliffords Tower, York

Above: Clifford's Tower was enclosed within a military prison compound until 1934.
Below: The Ouse, viewed from Skeldergate Bridge.

This is actually the second castle to stand here: the original structure burned down in 1190 under appalling circumstances when the city's Jewish population sought refuge from an anti-semitic mob.

The stone tower you see today was completed between 1250-75, and almost immediately began to subside – the vast crack running from top to bottom on the eastern face was first noticed in the 1350s. Originally the tower had a roof, but this blew off following a gunpowder accident in 1684. There's not a lot left to see inside, but the views from the battlements are spectacular.

Norman castles were built to a motte (mound) and bailey (courtyard) design; though the bailey of York's castle was replaced by the elegant trio of Georgian buildings on the other three sides of the lawn.

Below: 'York in the Fifteenth Century'– a reconstruction painting of York by Edwin Ridsdale Tate (1862 – 1922), architect & antiquary. Clifford's Tower with its moat dominates the foreground. On the opposite side of the river is Baile Hill, the former 'motte & bailey' castle. *York Mansion House/York Museums Trust*

To the right is the Crown Court, designed in 1773 by York's most celebrated 18th century architect, John Carr. The accommodation in the buildings opposite was not quite as palatial as the exteriors suggest; as both were originally prisons. They now contain the Castle Museum, the highlight of which is Kirkgate; a cobbled reconstruction of Victorian York laid out in the former exercise yard.

You can also visit the condemned cell where the highwayman Dick Turpin spent his final night before being taken to the gallows at York's historic racecourse, the Knavesmire. John Carr not only built the law courts and the prison, he designed the grandstand on the Knavesmire as well; giving condemned criminals a view they may not have appreciated of three of his finest creations in turn.

Top: Fairfax House designed by John Carr 1762.
Above: John Carr's grandstand at the Knavesmire racecourse, completed in 1754 but now sadly demolished.
Below: The Debtors' Prison (now part of the Castle Museum) was constructed between 1701-05. Affluent inmates could rent a suite of rooms at the top; common felons were kept in chains at the bottom.

CONCLUSION

So what if a 15th century visitor were to be propelled through the ages and set down in 21st century York? How much might seem familiar and how much would have changed?

Though the suburbs have expanded, the snickleways and medieval street pattern remain practically unaltered. The walls are (mostly) still intact and the Minster continues to dominate the skyline, though our medieval visitor might be a little dismayed at the ruined state of St Mary's Abbey.

We still have our love-hate relationship with the rivers. The Ouse and Foss brought trade and prosperity; but also Vikings and, more recently, devastating floods in which William the Conqueror's moat unexpectedly reappeared. But a medieval merchant would certainly recognise the Shambles, which still contains a shop known for its award-winning sausages, as well as two excellent bakeries and the longest-established Italian restaurant in York. In other words, York is not an empty heritage exhibit, but a busy, provincial city where you are as likely to rub shoulders with locals as with your fellow tourists.

Top: Clifford's Tower reflected in the floods of December 2015.
Centre: The Ouse in summer.
Left: A rainbow strikes the King's Arms, the most frequently flooded pub in the city.
Right: Now mainly used by pleasure boats, King's Staith has been York's principal quay from Viking times onwards.

Six million KitKats are still manufactured here every day, though it now says Nestlé on the packet. York station remains a significant hub on the East Coast line. But as we have seen over the course of this walk, the story of York has been shaped by one invading force following another – whether they be Romans, Vikings, railwaymen or multi-national confectionary firms.

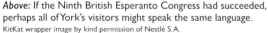

Above: If the Ninth British Esperanto Congress had succeeded, perhaps all of York's visitors might speak the same language.
KitKat wrapper image by kind permission of Nestlé S.A.

Now we have visitors from every part of the globe in what has grown to become the most decisive conquest of all – a welcome, benign invasion that we hope will continue into the next century and beyond.

47